Charge into Reading

Decodable Reader
with literacy activities

decodable

ĕ

Ten Hens
Short E

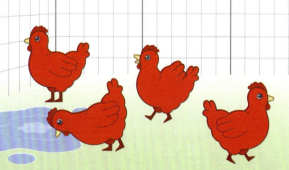

Brooke Vitale • Katarzyna Jasinska

CHARGE MOMMY
BOOKS
Riverside, CT

For information address contact@chargemommybooks.com
or visit chargemommybooks.com.

Printed in China
ISBN: 978-1-955947-18-3
10 9 8 7

Designed by Lindsay Broderick
Created in consultation with literacy specialist Marisa Ware, MSEd

Publisher's Cataloging-in-Publication Data
Names: Vitale, Brooke, author. | Jasinska, Katarzyna, illustrator.
Title: Ten hens : short e decodable reader / Brooke Vitale, Katarzyna Jasinska.
Description: Riverside, CT : Charge Mommy Books, 2022.| Illustrated early reader. | Series: Charge into Reading. | Audience: Ages 4-6. | Summary: Introduces children to the short E sound. Includes eight pages of short E literacy activities at the end.
Identifiers: LCCN 2022901738 | ISBN 9781955947183 (pbk.)
Subjects: LCSH: Hens -- Juvenile fiction. | Reading -- Code emphasis approaches -- Juvenile literature. | Reading -- Phonetic method -- Juvenile literature. | Readers (Primary). | BISAC: JUVENILE FICTION / Animals / Farm Animals. | JUVENILE FICTION / Concepts / Sounds. | JUVENILE FICTION / Readers / Beginner.
Classification: LCC PZ7.1 V59 Ten 2022 | DDC E V59te--dc22
LC record available at https://lccn.loc.gov/2022901738

Jen met a hen.

The hen was red.

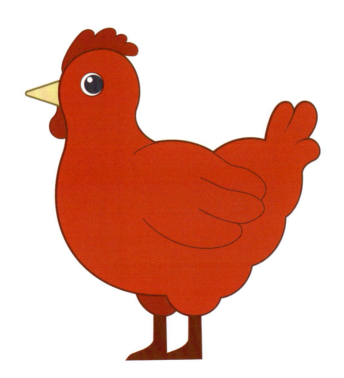

Jen pet the hen.

Jen fed the hen.

Jen led the hen
to a pen.

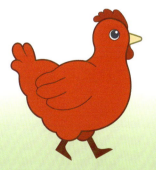

Jen met ten red hens.

Jen pet ten red hens.

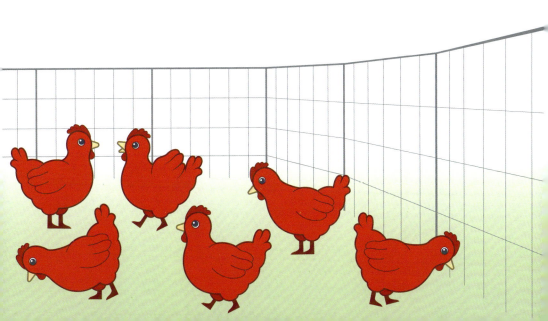

Jen fed ten hens.

Jen fell in the pen.

The pen is wet.
Jen is wet.

Ted met Jen.

Jen let Ted help.

Ted fell in the pen!

Oh, Ted!

Let's Talk Literacy!

Read the sentence below. Then circle the picture that matches the sentence.

Jen fed the hen.

Let's Talk Literacy!

Say the name of each picture below.
As you speak, **tap out** the sounds
for each word. Then **write the letter**
for each sound in the box.

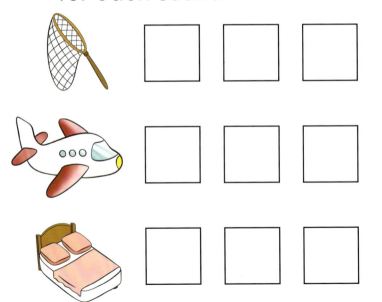

Let's Talk Literacy!

Say the name of each picture below. Then circle the words that make a **short E sound**.

Answers: well, net, hen, web, bed

Let's Talk Literacy!

Say the name of the picture in each row. Then circle the word in each row that is part of the same **word family**.

hen

let set men bed new

fell

met well net ten fed

met

wed sell vet gel let

Let's Talk Literacy!

Say the word. Then look at the picture to figure out its **rhyming word**. Change the first letter of the word to make the new word, and write it on the line.

Word	Change to	New word
tell		_____
set		_____
den		_____

Let's Talk Literacy!

Look at each picture below. Then read the words below each picture. **Circle the word** that matches the picture.

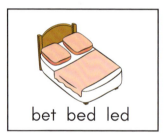

bet bed led

hen men hem

bed web well

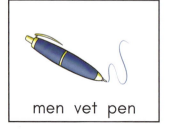

men vet pen

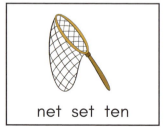

net set ten

wet bell well

Let's Talk Literacy!

The word **den** is part of the **-EN word family**. Name the pictures below. Then circle the ones that are also part of the -EN word family.

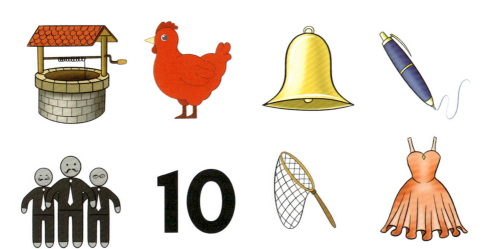

Let's Talk Literacy!

Say the name of each picture below. Then draw a line to the letter that makes the **first sound** in the word.

Nn   Bb   Tt   Pp   Hh   Ss